Off with Their Heads
An Antifascist Coloring Book for Adults of All Ages
N.O. Bonzo

This edition © PM Press 2020

PM Press
PO Box 23912
Oakland, CA 94623
www.pmpress.org

ISBN (paperback): 9781629638591
ISBN (ebook): 9781629638607
10 9 8 7 6 5 4 3 2 1
Printed in the USA

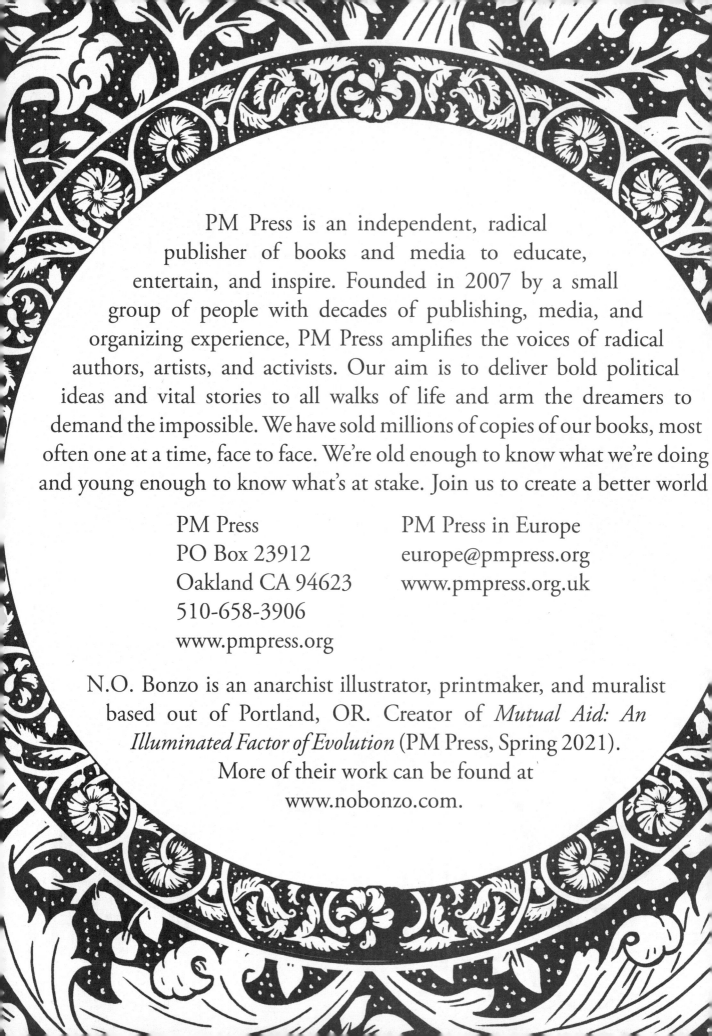

PM Press is an independent, radical publisher of books and media to educate, entertain, and inspire. Founded in 2007 by a small group of people with decades of publishing, media, and organizing experience, PM Press amplifies the voices of radical authors, artists, and activists. Our aim is to deliver bold political ideas and vital stories to all walks of life and arm the dreamers to demand the impossible. We have sold millions of copies of our books, most often one at a time, face to face. We're old enough to know what we're doing and young enough to know what's at stake. Join us to create a better world

PM Press
PO Box 23912
Oakland CA 94623
510-658-3906
www.pmpress.org

PM Press in Europe
europe@pmpress.org
www.pmpress.org.uk

N.O. Bonzo is an anarchist illustrator, printmaker, and muralist based out of Portland, OR. Creator of *Mutual Aid: An Illuminated Factor of Evolution* (PM Press, Spring 2021). More of their work can be found at www.nobonzo.com.

Friends of PM

These are indisputably momentous times—the financial system is melting down globally and the Empire is stumbling. Now more than ever there is a vital need for radical ideas.

In the twelve years since its founding—and on a mere shoestring—PM Press has risen to the formidable challenge of publishing and distributing knowledge and entertainment for the struggles ahead. With over 500 releases to date, we have published an impressive and stimulating array of literature, art, music, politics, history, and culture. Using every available medium, we've succeeded in connecting those hungry for ideas and information to those putting them into practice.

Friends of PM allows you to directly help impact, amplify, and revitalize the discourse and actions of radical writers, filmmakers, and artists. It provides us with a stable foundation from which we can build upon our early successes and provides a much-needed subsidy for the materials that can't necessarily pay their own way. You can help make that happen—and receive every new title automatically delivered to your door once a month—by joining as a Friend of PM Press.

Here are your options:

  $15 a month: Get 3 e-Books emailed to you plus 50% discount on all webstore purchases.
  $30 a month: Get all books and pamphlets plus 50% discount on all webstore purchases
  $40 a month: Get all PM Press releases (including CDs and DVDs) plus 50% discount on all webstore purchases
  $100 a month: Superstar - Everything plus PM merchandise, free downloads, and 50% discount on all webstore purchases

For those who can't afford the shelf space, but can afford the solidarity and support, we're introducing **Sustainer Rates** at $100, $50, $2 $15, $10 and $5. Sustainers get a free PM Press T-shirt and a 50% discount on all purchases from our website.

Your Visa or Mastercard will be billed once a month, until you tell us to stop. Or until our efforts succeed in bringing the revolution around Or the financial meltdown of Capital makes plastic redundant. Whichever comes first.